Internal Reflections Volume One

by
Alan John Hewitt

Modern Ned

est. 2013

Publishing

Dedicated to making great art

1

AJH

AJH

4

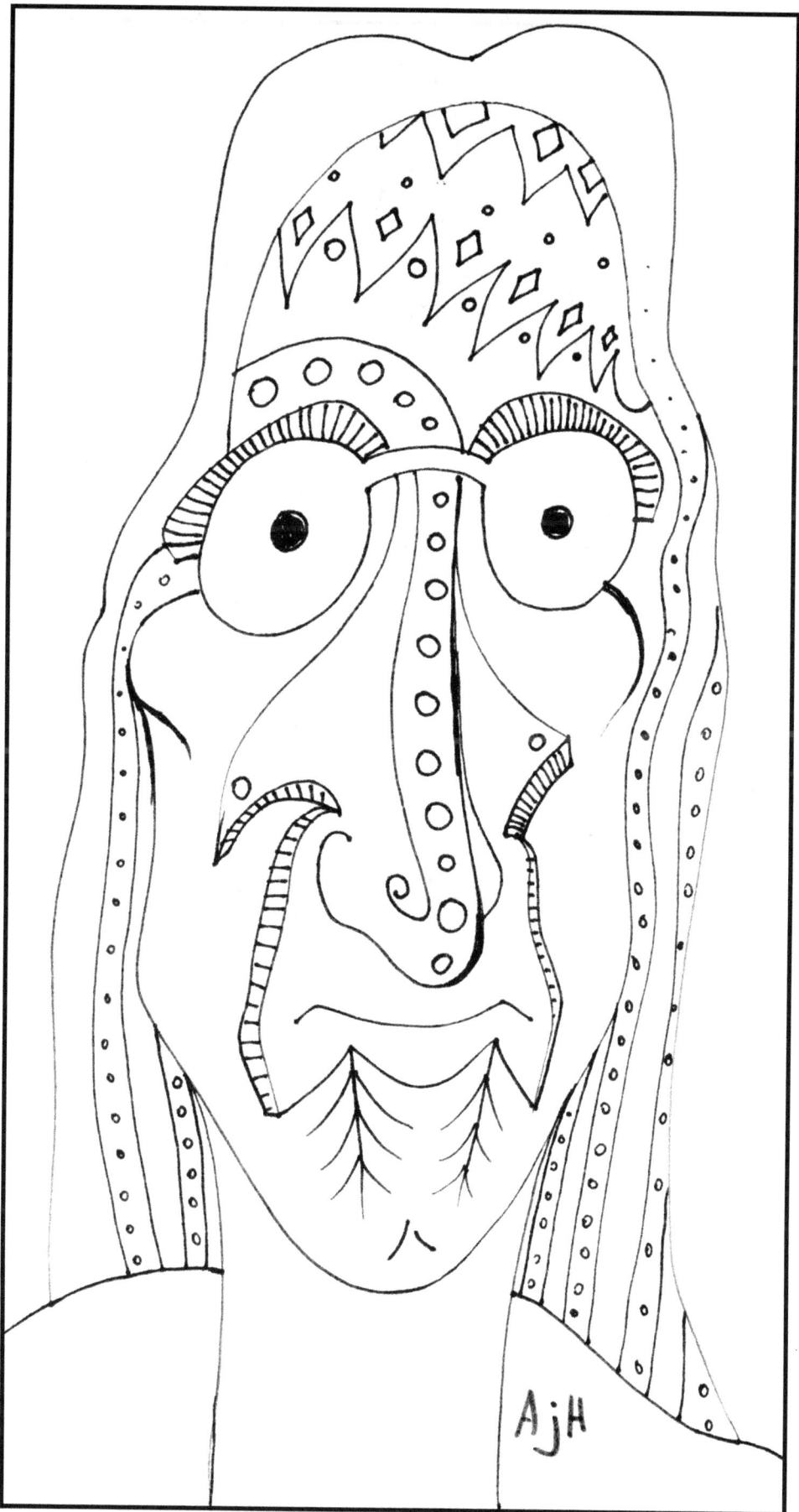

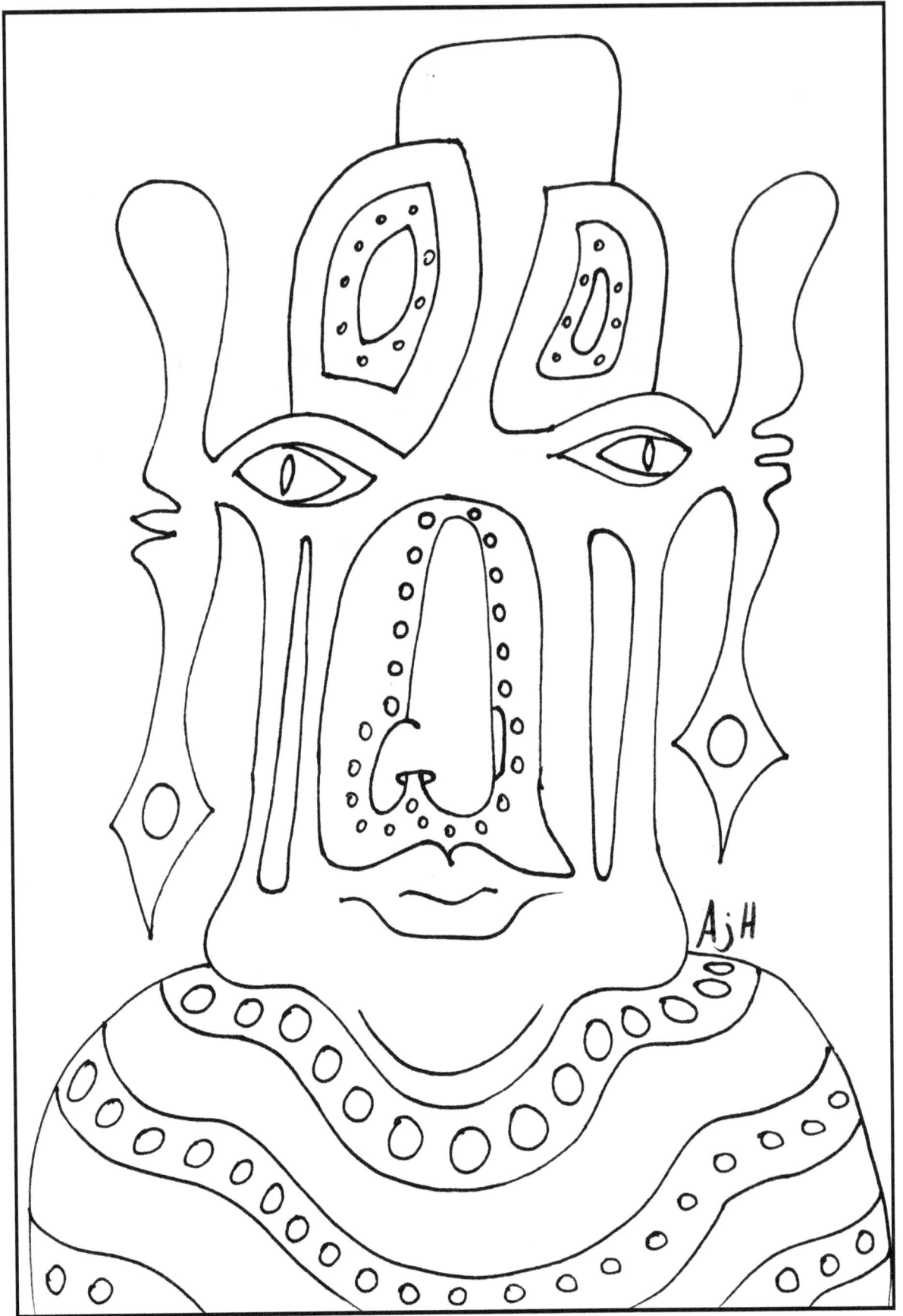

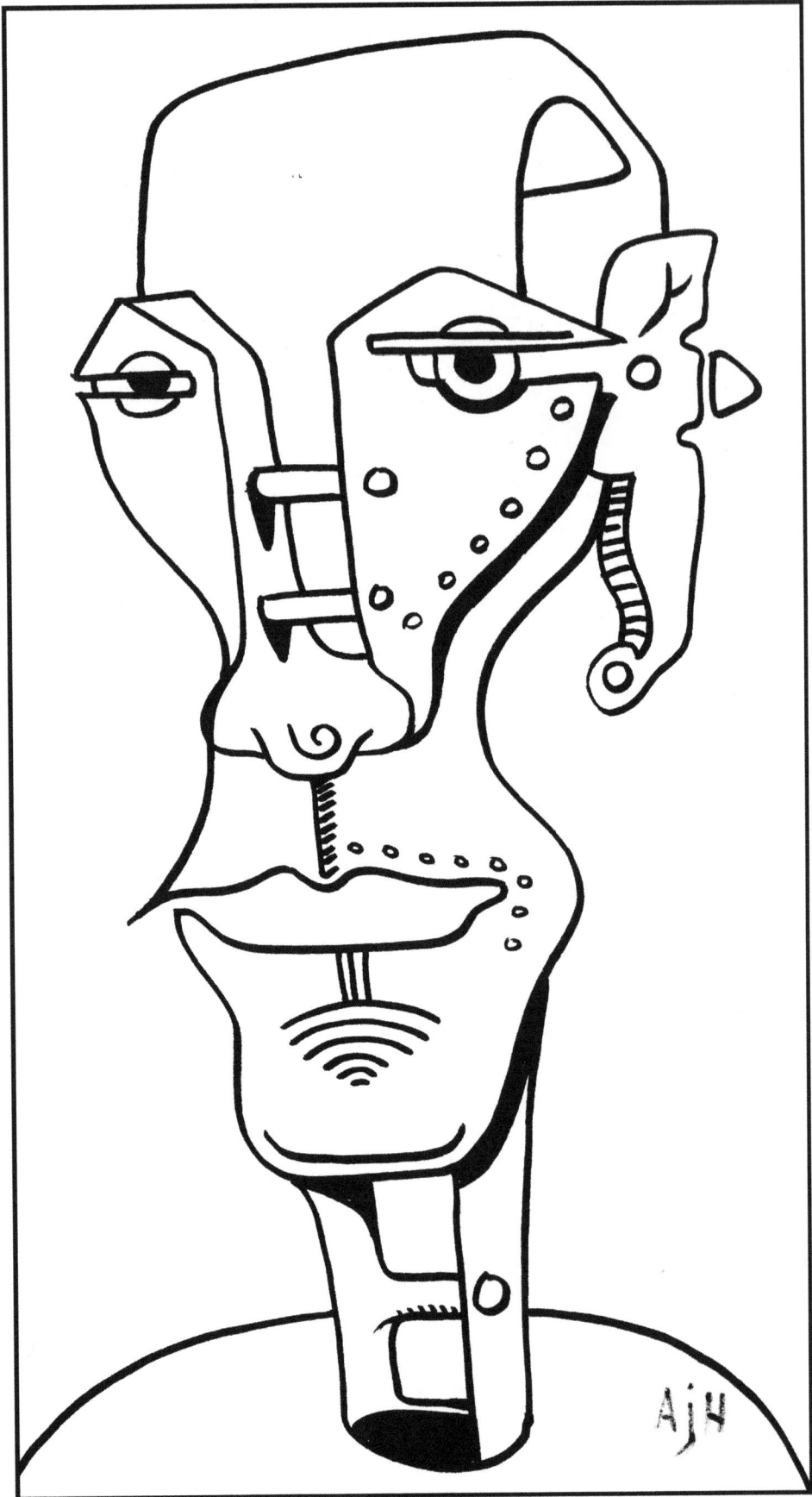

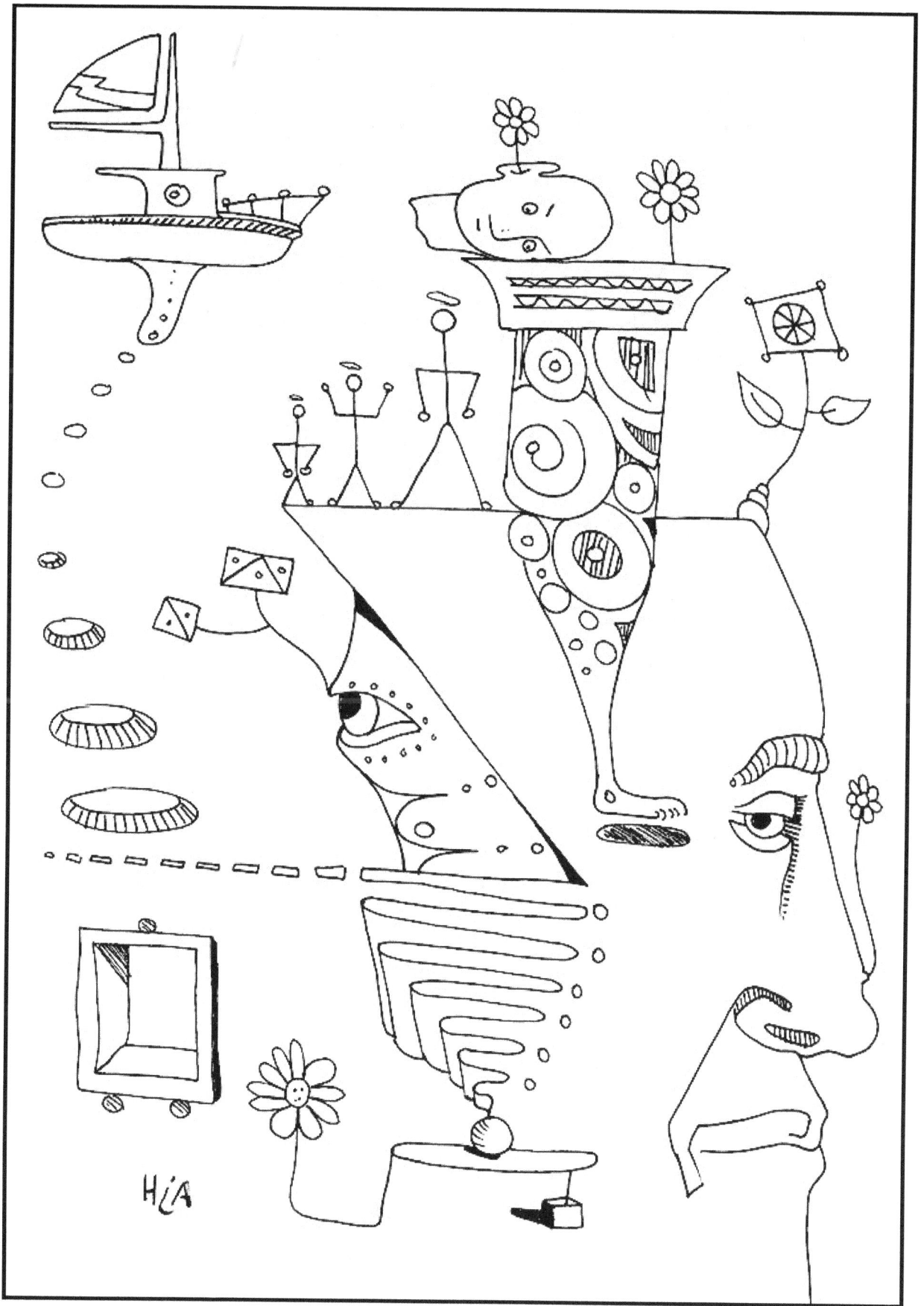

HiA

13

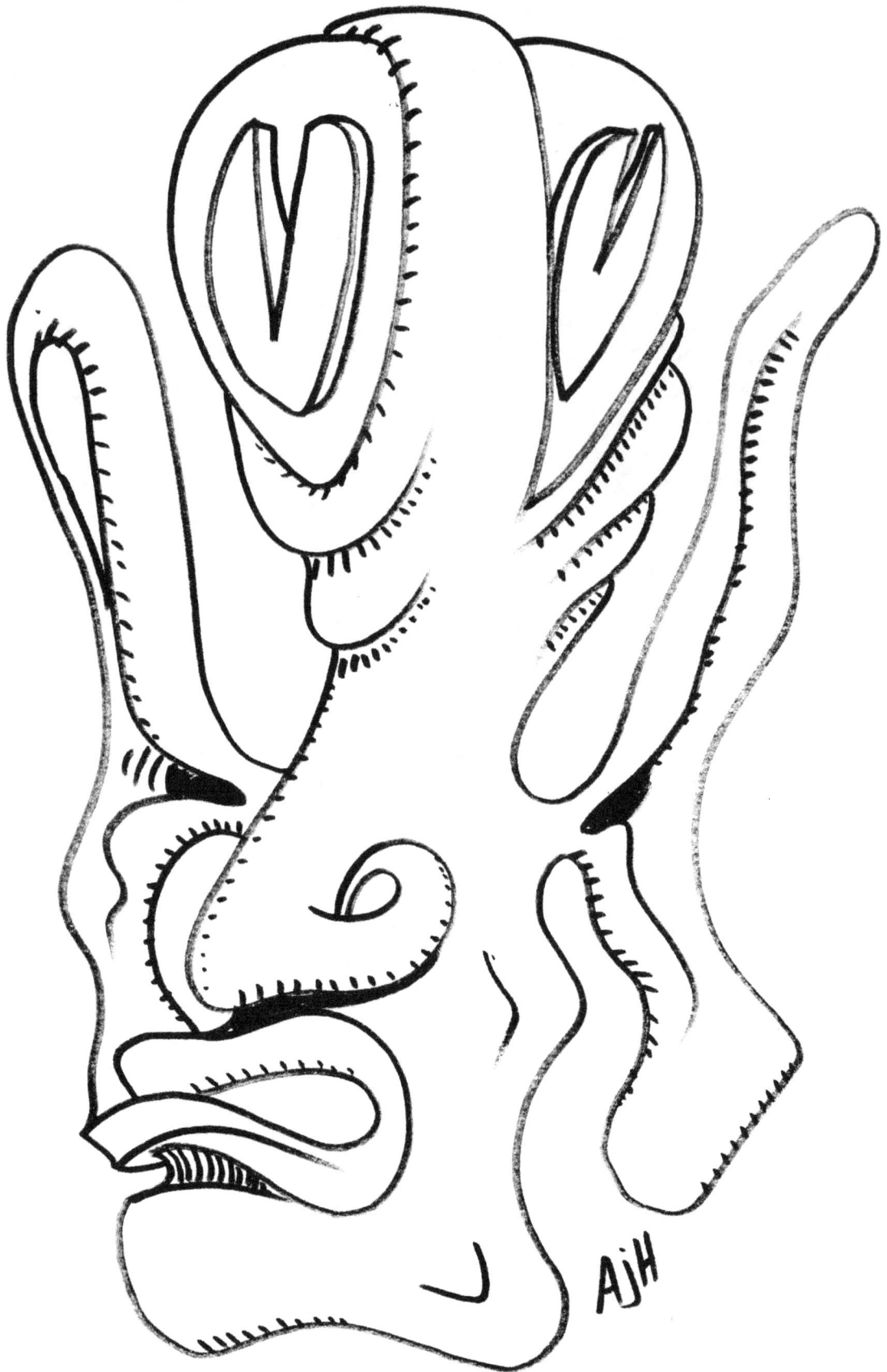

14

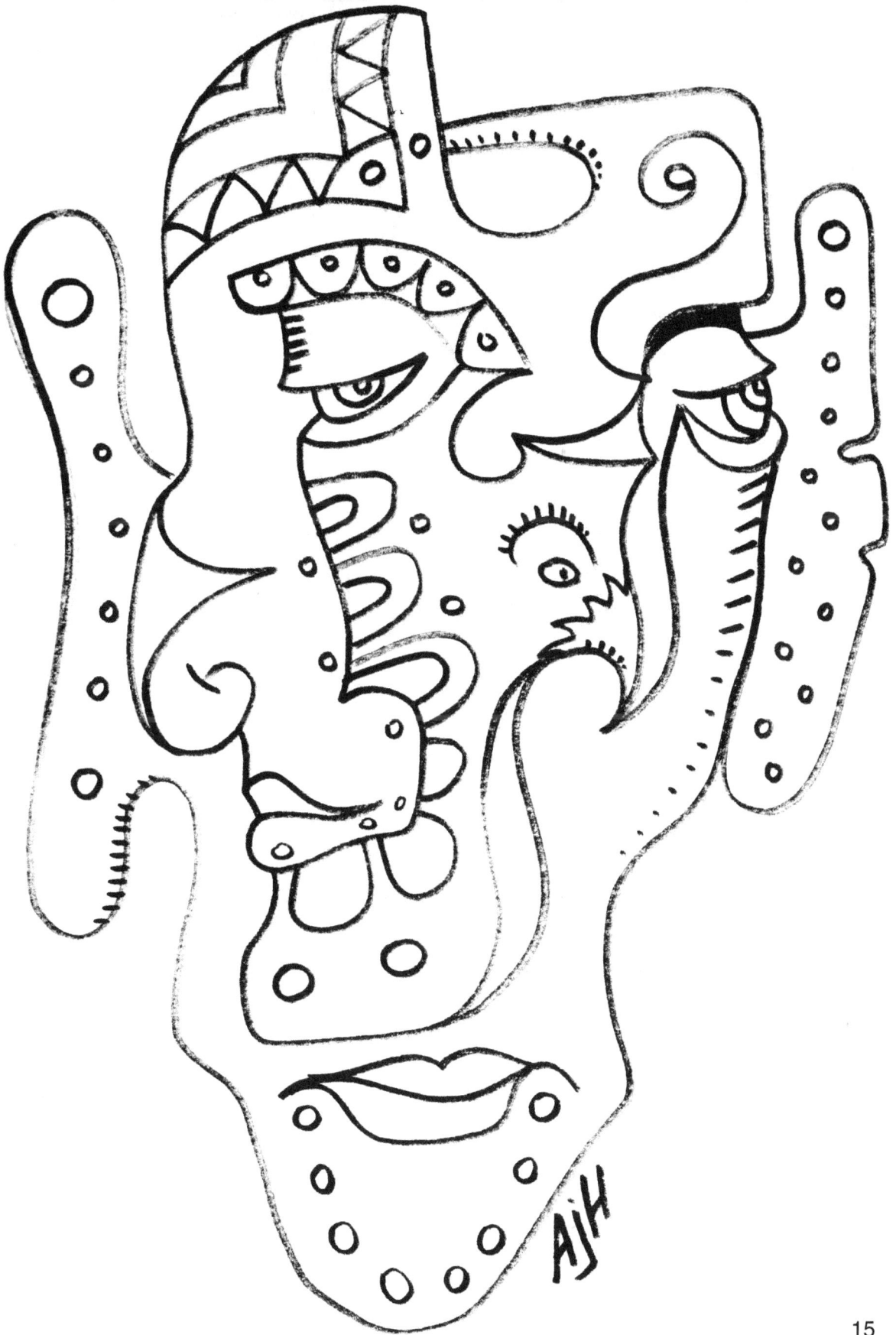

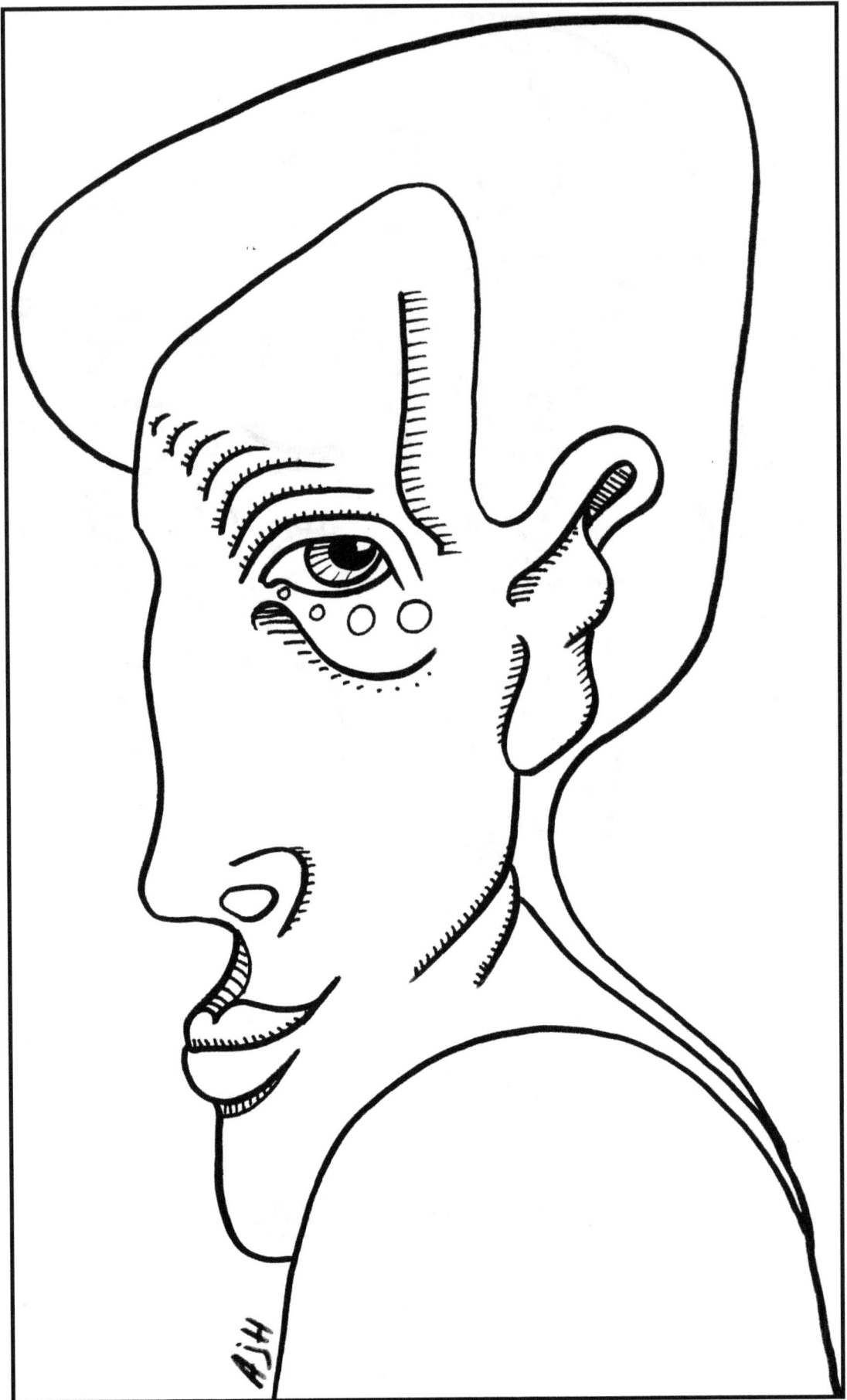

16

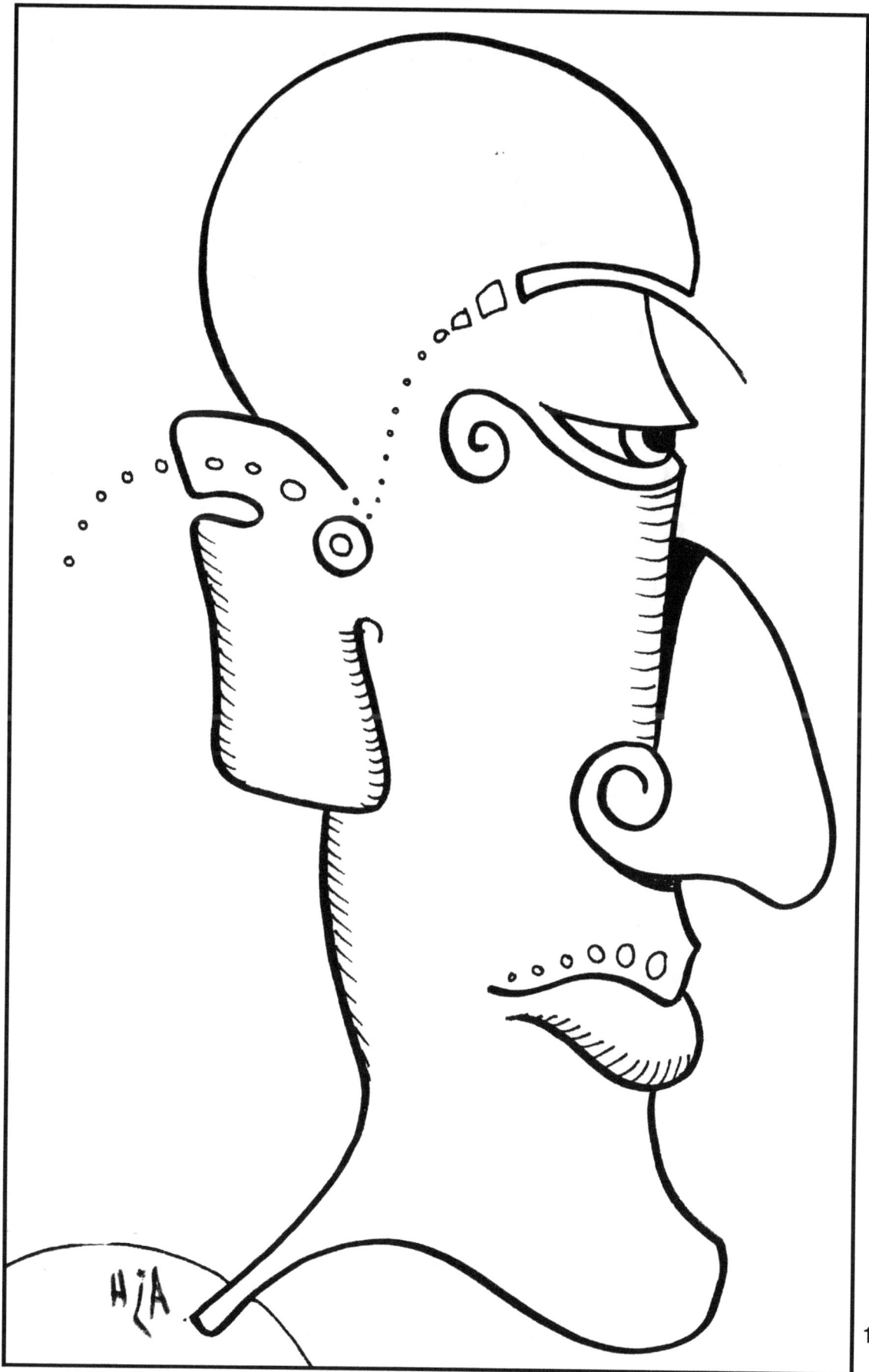

HÍA

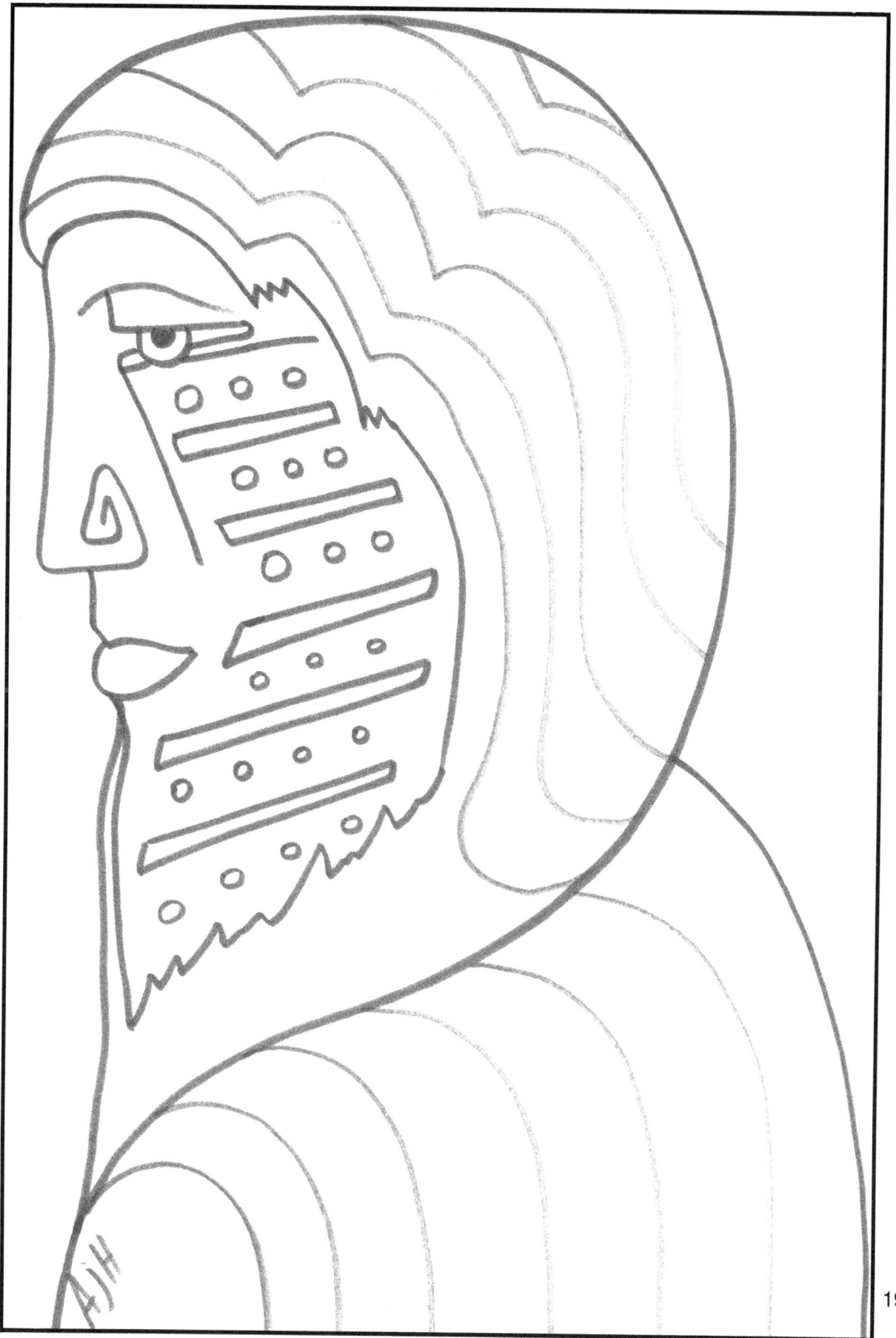

19

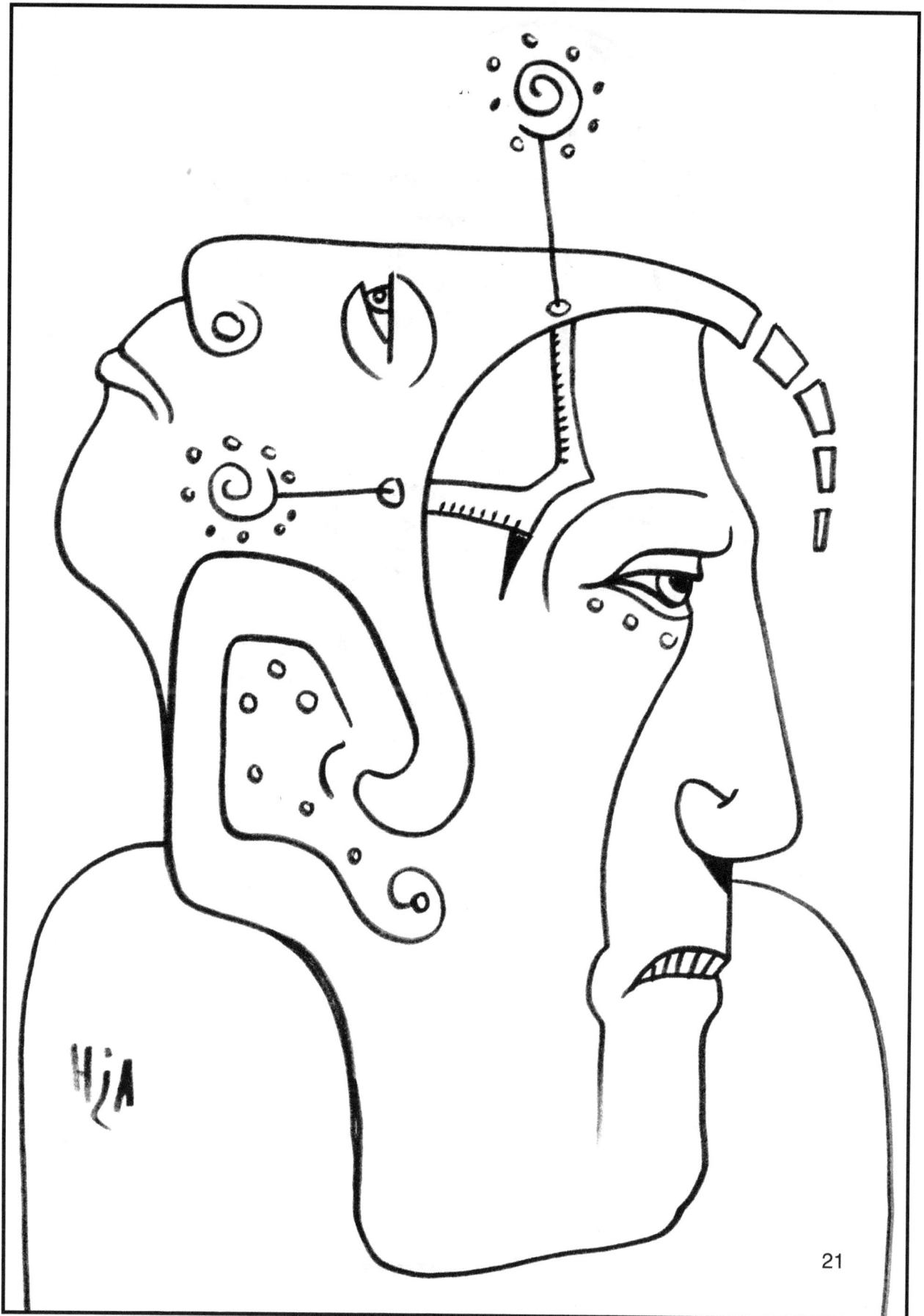

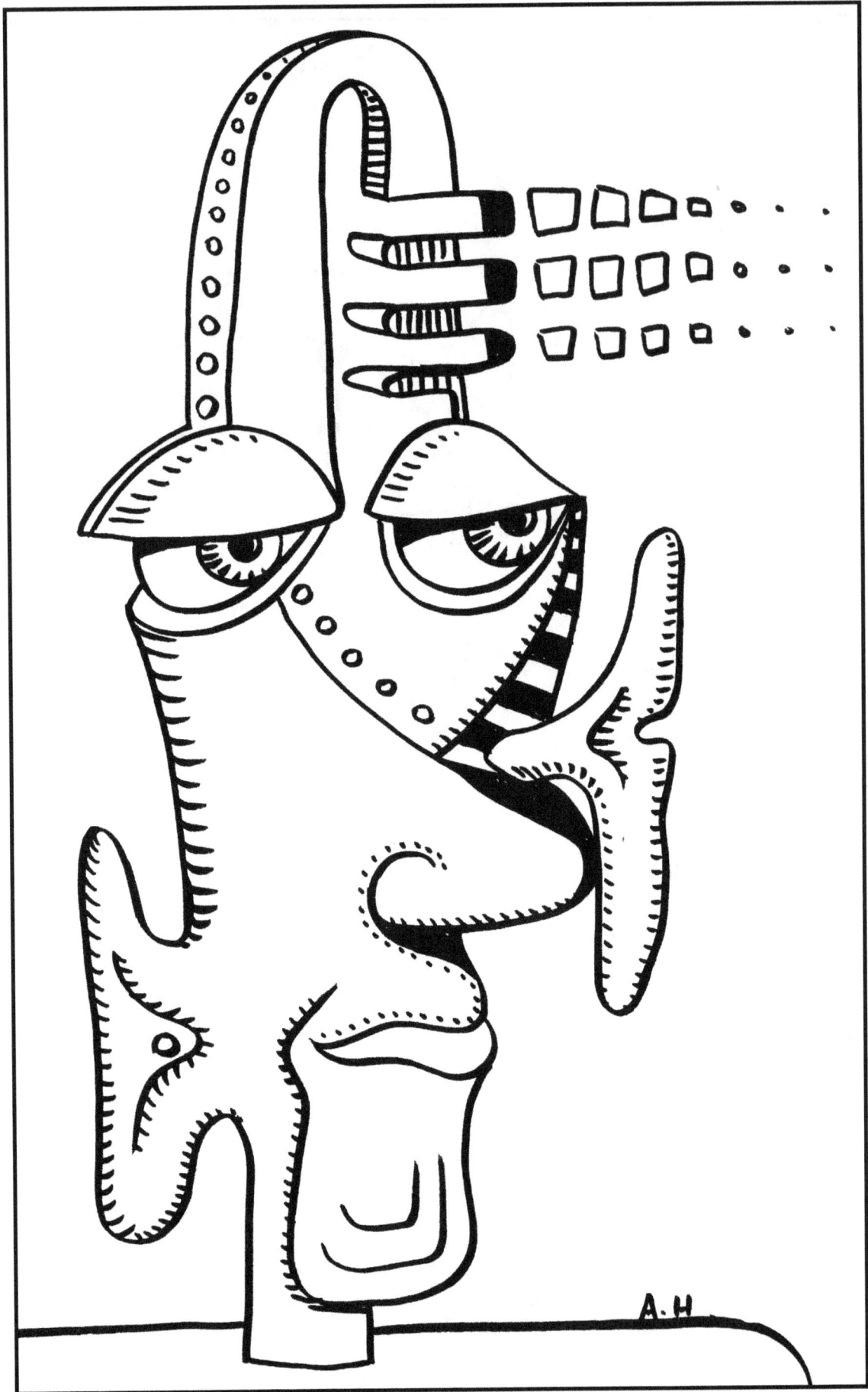

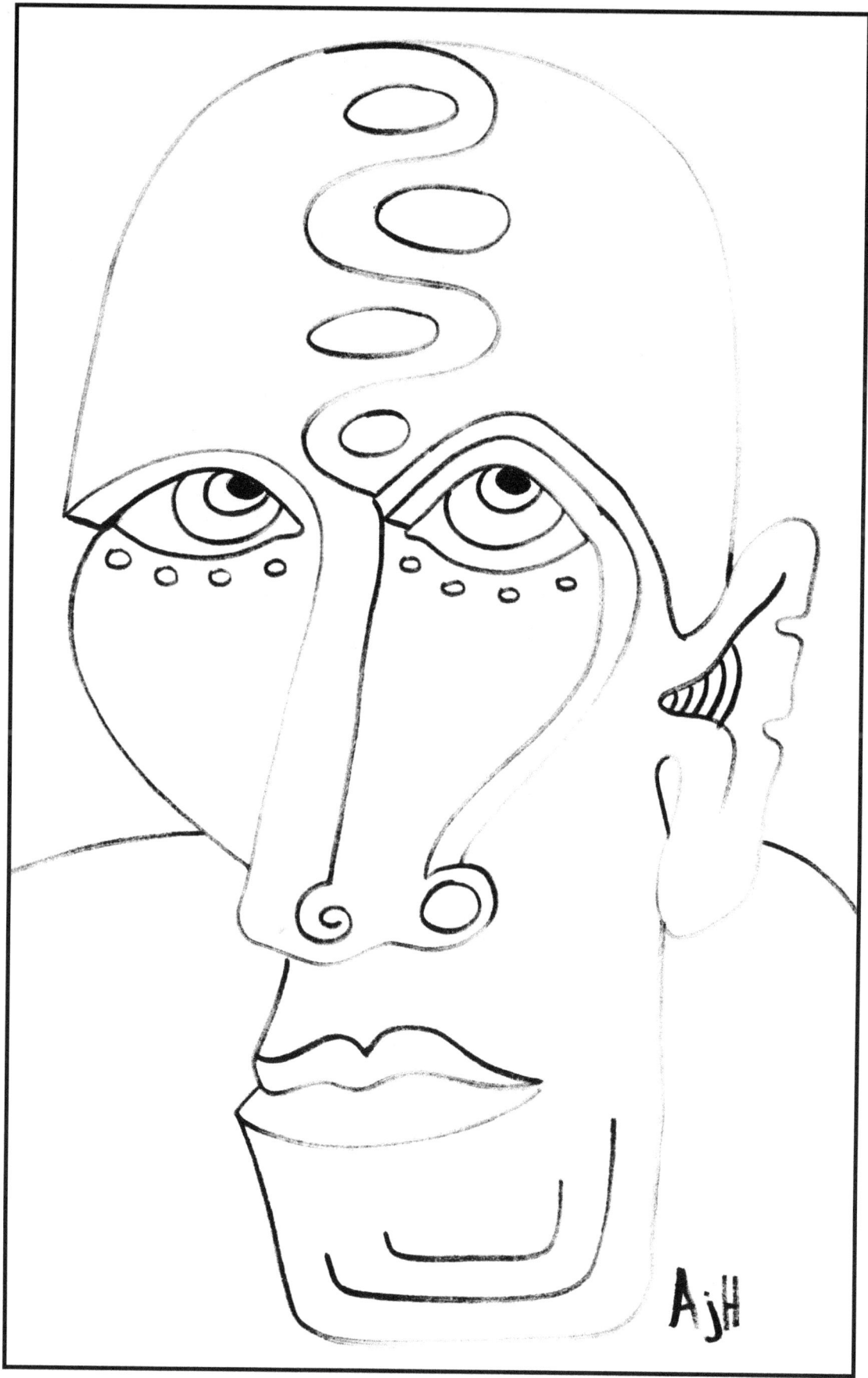

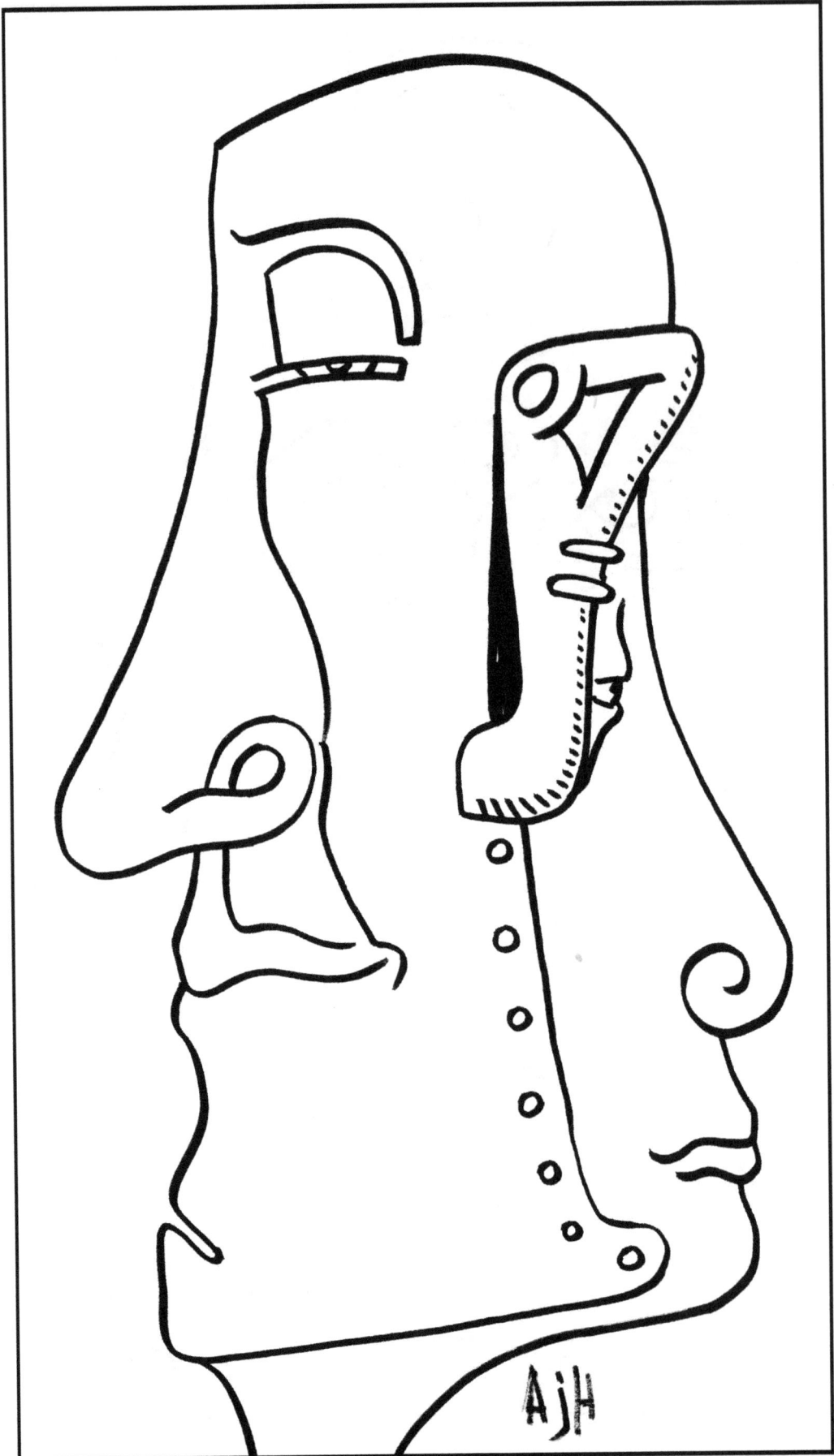

24

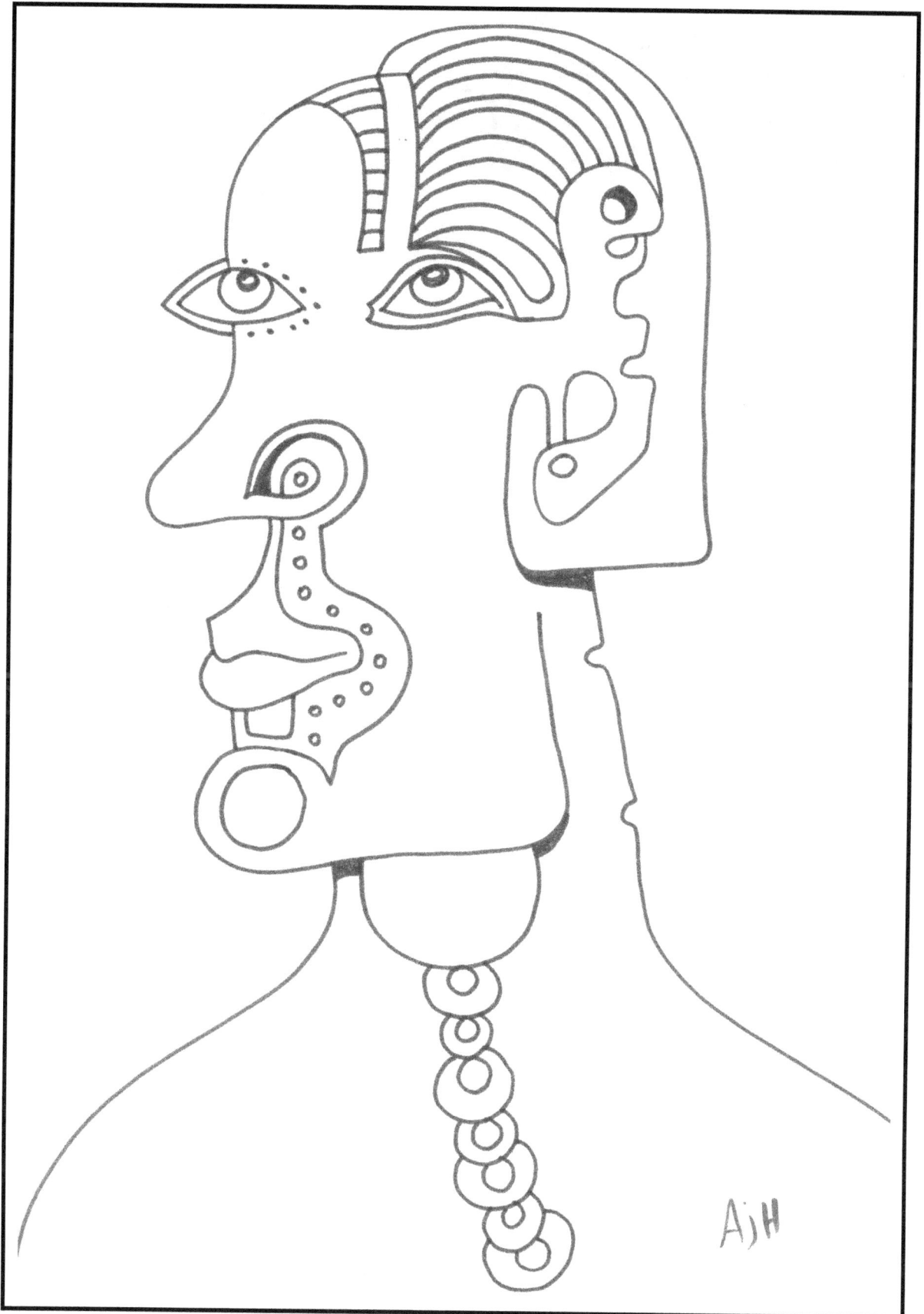

AJH

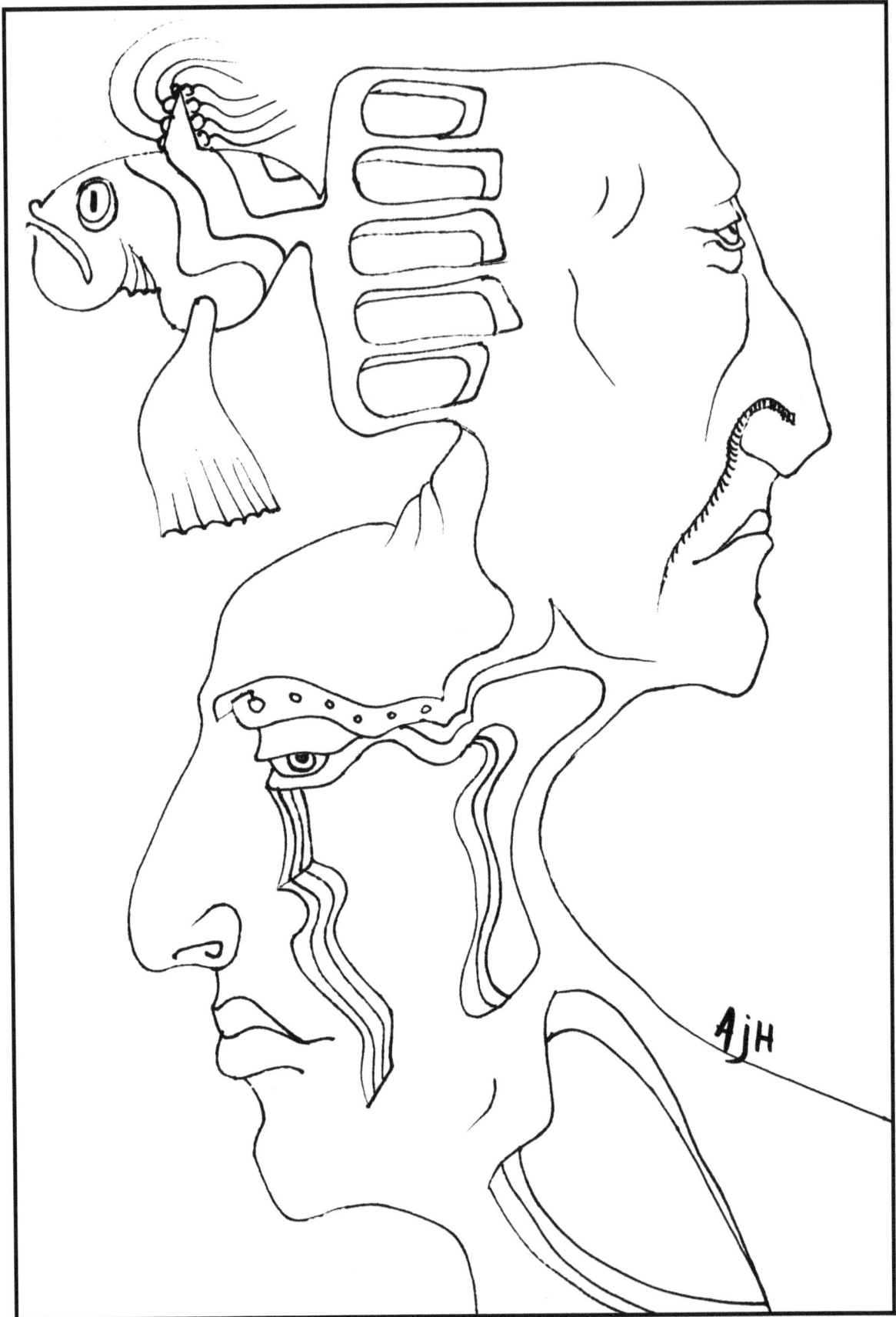

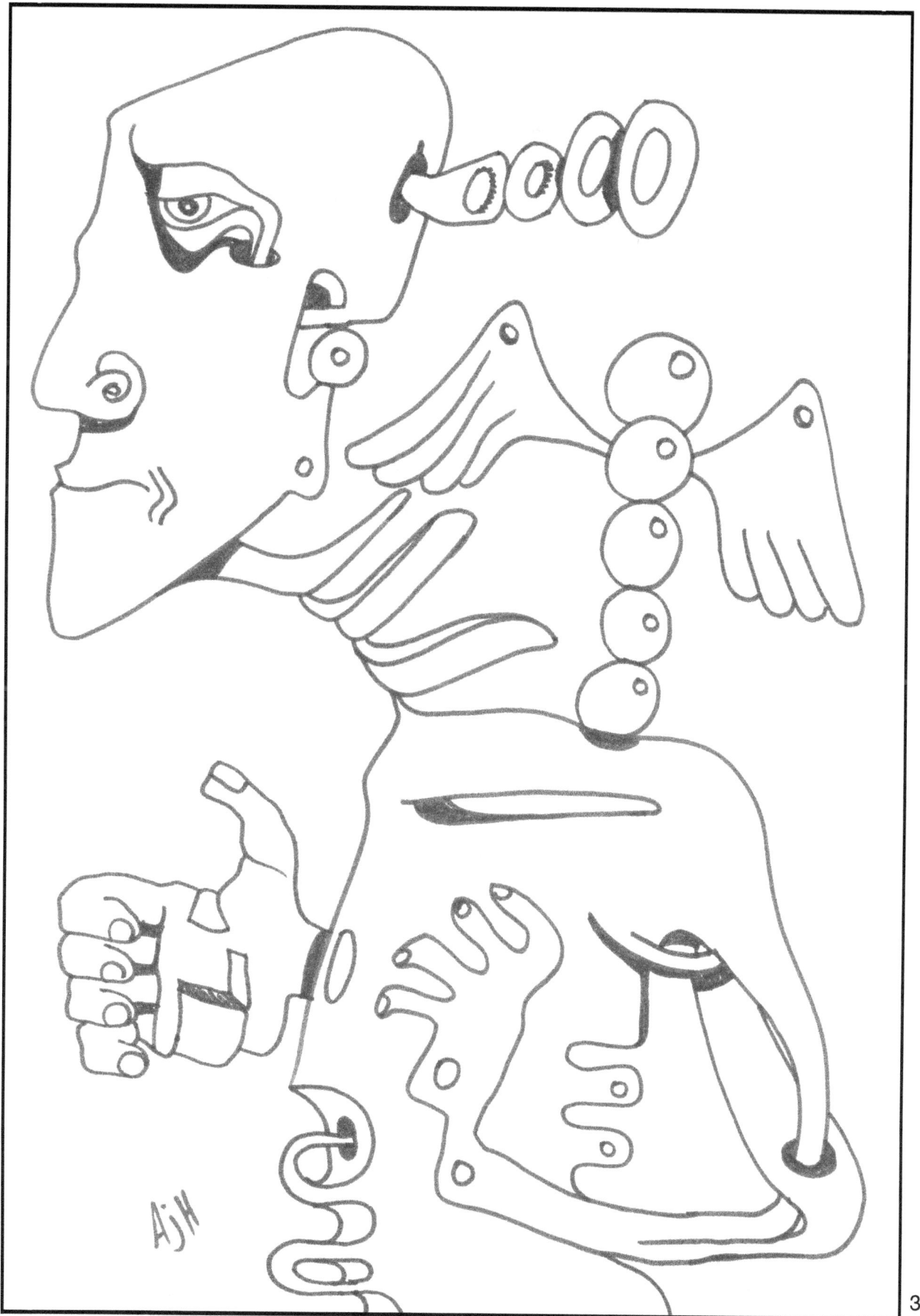

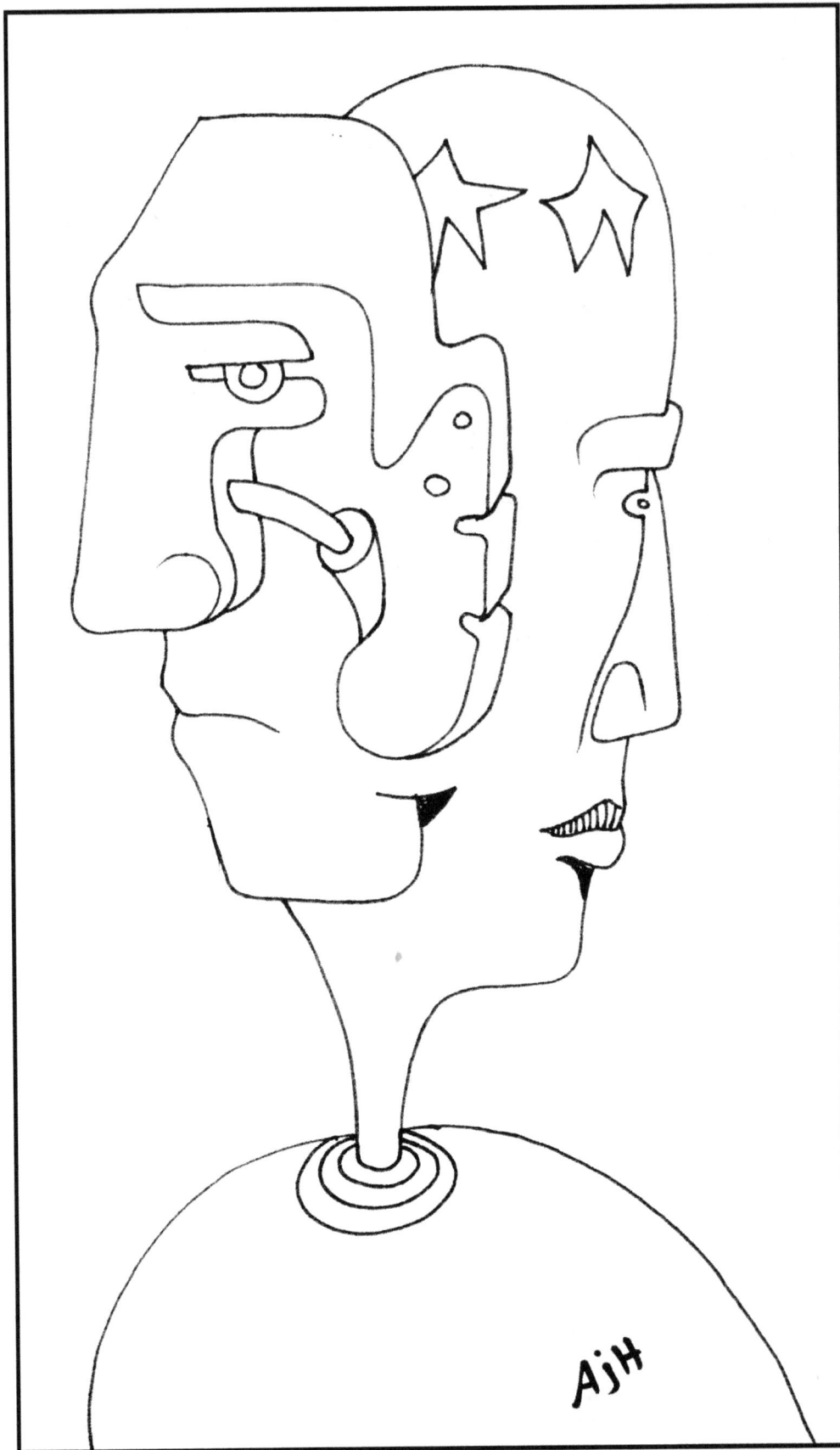

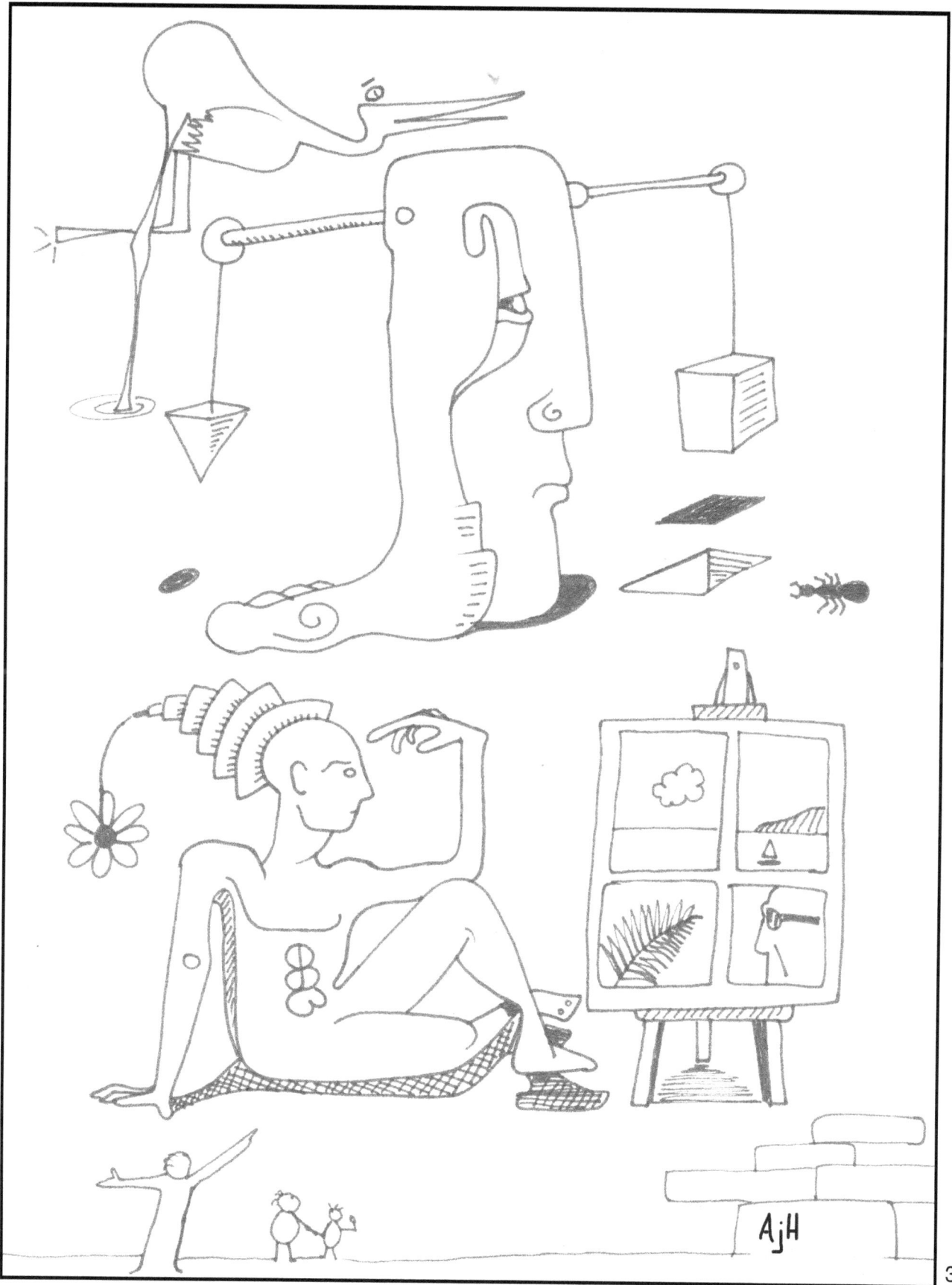

AjH

Modern Ned Publishing
Dedicated to making great art

Sign up for our weekly **Arts Letter**

New idea's and Original thoughts
Get full colour images from the
"The Internal Highway"
Series published weekly
before publication on social media.
Get it all when you sign up.

signup@modernnedpublishing.ca

We look forward to hearing from you.

All images are the intellectual property
of the Artist
Alan John Hewitt
Internal Reflections volume one ISBN : 978-0-9920060-6-8
Published by
Modern Ned Publishing
8 - 1010 Ellery Street
Esquimalt BC Canada
V9A-6Z8